To Rita

Tales from Croydon Minster

David Morgan

I do hope you enjoy the tales

David

Published by
Filament Publishing Ltd
16, Croydon Road, Beddington, Croydon,
Surrey, CR0 4PA, United Kingdom.
+44(0)20 8688 2598
www.filamentpublishing.com

Photographs by David Morgan, Steve O'Sullivan,
Adrian Gerrish and Chris Day

ISBN 978-1-911425-00-7

Printed by IngramSpark

About the Author

David Morgan

The author was born in Lowestoft, Suffolk but spent his years of study and teaching in South London. Recently retired after a successful 12-year headship in Croydon, David is now able to spend more time writing, researching local history and singing in the Croydon Minster choir. He leads tours of the church and the Whitgift Almshouses.

Table of Contents

MDCLX
MDCLXIII
OCTOGENARIUS
DEO REDDIDIT

Foreword

I have been the Vicar of Croydon for 22 years and I will be retiring at the end of June this year (2016). This foreward gives me a real opportunity to encourage you to come and see our magnificent building. A church, though, is nothing without the people associated with it. In this book, David highlights some of the stories of folk connected with our church in many different ways, and over very many years.

If you cannot come to our building, then we hope that these stories will give you a flavour of our position and our history, and that these insights will speak to you about what has happened here over the centuries. This church has held a special place in the lives of so many, and continues to do so today.

Canon Colin J Luke Boswell

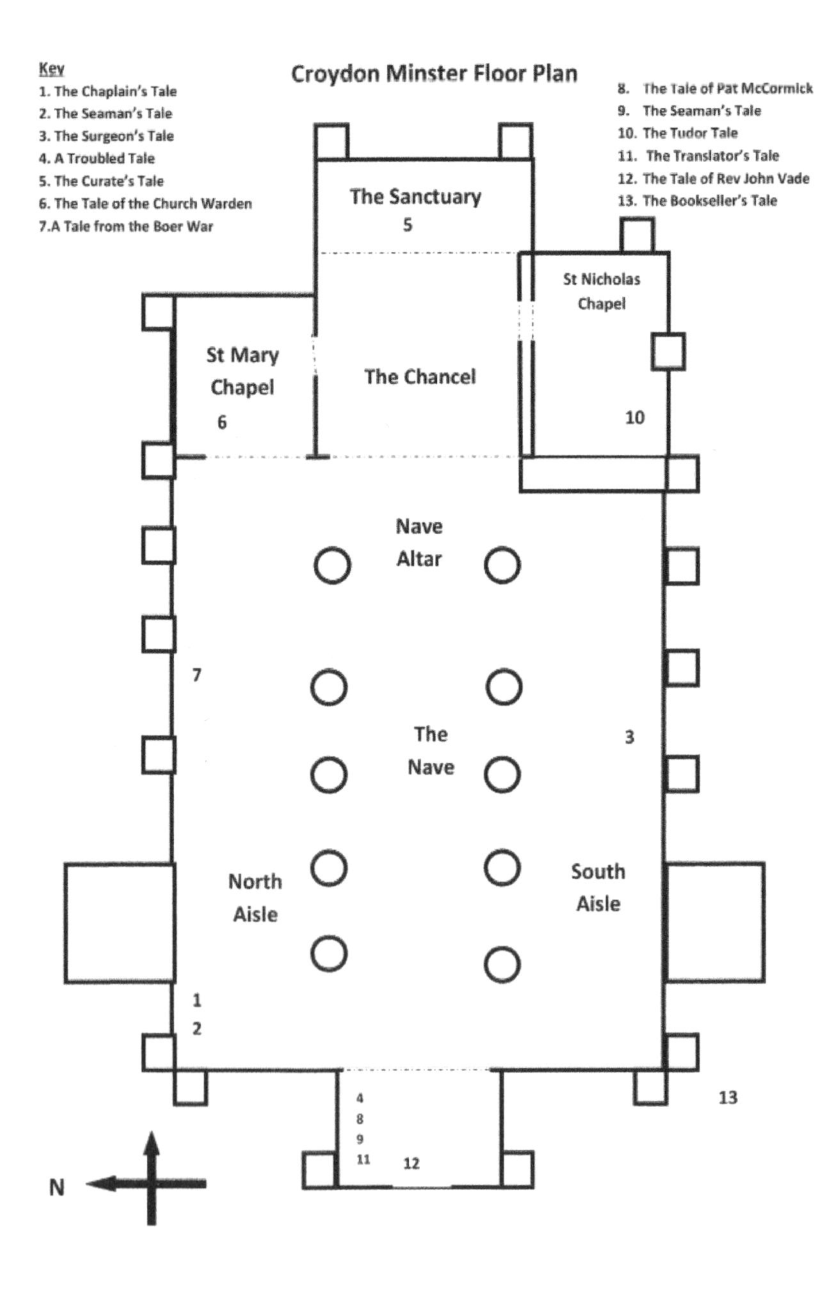
Croydon Minster Floor Plan
Key
1. The Chaplain's Tale
2. The Seaman's Tale
3. The Surgeon's Tale
4. A Troubled Tale
5. The Curate's Tale
6. The Tale of the Church Warden
7.A Tale from the Boer War
8. The Tale of Pat McCormick
9. The Seaman's Tale
10. The Tudor Tale
11. The Translator's Tale
12. The Tale of Rev John Vade
13. The Bookseller's Tale
The Sanctuary
5
St Nicholas Chapel
St Mary Chapel
The Chancel
6
10
Nave Altar
7
The Nave
3
North Aisle
South Aisle
1
2
4
8
9
11
12
13
N

About the Minster

Croydon Minster has a long and distinguished history. It is believed to have been founded in Saxon times, since there is a record of "a priest of Croydon" in 960, although the first record of a church building is in Domesday Book (1086). The church has had close links with the Archbishops of Canterbury who had a Palace in Croydon. Much of that building still stands next to the Minster and is now the Old Palace of John Whitgift School. Six Archbishops of Canterbury are buried in the Minster and many more would have worshipped here.

Kings and queens were regular visitors to the archbishops at Croydon - visits by Henry VII, Henry VIII and Queen Elizabeth I are all well documented. Ten bishops have been consecrated here and the church continues to be regularly used for ordinations and major diocesan and civic services, as well as for the daily parish worship.

In its final medieval form, the Minster was mainly a Perpendicular-style structure, but this was severely damaged by fire in 1867, following which only the tower, south porch and outer walls remained. Under the direction of Sir George Gilbert Scott, the church was rebuilt, incorporating the remains and essentially following the design of the medieval building, and was reconsecrated in 1870. It still contains several important monuments and fittings saved from the old church.

The West Tower

The main entrance to the church is through the west door beneath the predominantly medieval tower, 125 feet high to the top of the pinnacles. Above the west door can be seen the arms of Archbishops Courtenay and Chicheley, who were mainly responsible for the building in the 14th and 15th centuries.

The Nave

The church is almost 150 feet in length from east to west. The nave (the main body of the church) is 92 feet high and has a fine open timberwork roof supported by angel corbels. The original eagle lectern, a fine specimen of fifteenth-century brass work, with small lions at its feet, is still in regular use.

The nave is one of the few such pre-Reformation lecterns remaining in this country. The Victorian pulpit, ornamented by carved figures of saints, is by Thompson of Peterborough.

The North Aisle

There are a number of medieval remains in the north aisle. These include an ornamental recess, said formerly to have been a holy water stoup (a basin for holy water), and a larger recess (possibly for a tomb) containing the remains of a double piscina (in which the communion chalice would have been washed) and a late fifteenth-century altar tomb. The distinguished American-born artist, John Singleton Copley R.A. (1737-1815), is commemorated by a plaque. On the same wall may be seen a brass inscription to Elys Davy (died 1455), who founded the nearby almshouses, and brass shields which formed part of a memorial to Thomas Heron (died 1544).

The Chancel

The chancel is richly decorated, notably the waggon-shaped oak roof, supported by angel corbels, some of them gilded and holding musical instruments. The pointed arch in the north wall is formed of early English fragments, below which is a Victorian fresco of the feeding of the 5,000. The east wall is filled by a large Perpendicular-style window, containing fine glass depicting New Testament scenes by one of the best known Victorian firms, Clayton and Bell; and, beneath, a rich alabaster reredos (the ornamental screen behind the High Altar) carved with reliefs of the nativity, crucifixion and resurrection. The Victorian altar frontal has recently been restored to its original splendour. In the south wall are elaborate piscina and sedilia (priests' seats), the latter incorporating painted roundels of three archbishops.

There are a number of brasses inside the chancel arch. William Heron (died 1562) and his wife are commemorated on the north side, while the large figure on the south side commemorates Gabriel Sylvester (died 1513) who was Master of Clare College, Cambridge and is depicted as a priest in vestments. The choir stalls feature some interesting and curious carvings on the bench ends, which repay closer study. To the north of the chancel is the Victorian organ, built by Hill & Son and whose oak case was decorated by J. Oldrid Scott. A second smaller organ, acquired recently from a village church in Hampshire, can be seen in the St. Nicholas Chapel. The church is a regular venue for recitals and concerts.

The St. Nicholas Chapel

Both side chapels are on the site of earlier chantry chapels (a chapel paid for by a patron for whom prayers would be said on his or her death). In the St. Nicholas or Bishop's Chapel is the large coloured monument to John Whitgift (died 1604), who was Archbishop of Canterbury during the reign of Elizabeth I and at the start of that of James I. Whitgift was a major local benefactor, who founded the old almshouses (dated 1596) which can still be seen in the town centre. Schools and the Whitgift shopping centre also perpetuate his name. Archbishop Whitgift's tomb shows him lying in prayer, surrounded by allegorical figures and cherubs. Next to it is a sixteenth-century carved tomb chest believed to be that of Hugh Warham, brother of another Archbishop. The memorial of Archbishop Wake (died 1736/7) was dedicated by his successor, Archbishop Runcie, in 1989.

The South Aisle

In the south aisle, behind iron railings, is the white marble monument (still slightly damaged) to Archbishop Sheldon, who founded the Sheldonian Theatre in Oxford and died in Croydon in 1677. Emblems of mortality are carved beneath his reclining figure. Nearby is another remnant of the brass to Thomas Heron (1544), depicting his daughters. Also in this wall are two small recesses, one though to be an aumbry with a piscina drain inserted, the other closer to the porch probably a former holy water stoup.

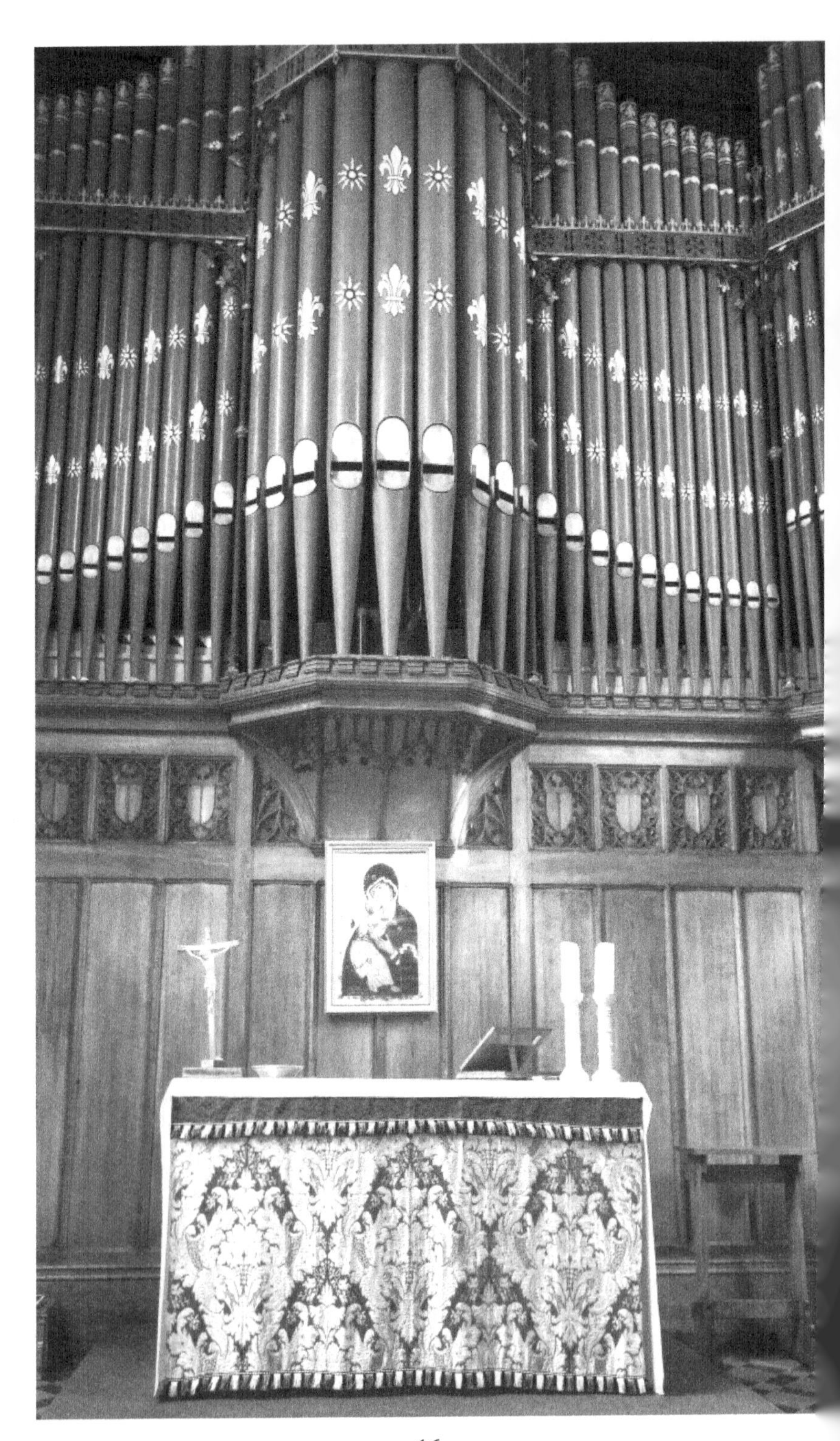

The south porch, with its parvise and original vaulting, dates from the fifteenth century, although this is not usually accessible (the exterior can, however, be seen from the memorial garden south of the church). The octagonal font is Victorian and has a very tall canopy, carved with figures of archbishops. West of the font is a restored tomb recess, and beneath the west window there are fragments from an old tomb (Nicholas Heron, 1568).

Dedication

The Minster, dedicated to St. John the Baptist, is the Mother Church of Croydon, and as the Civic Church plays an important role in the life of the borough. Over the years it has been involved in many developments in the fields of housing, education, counselling services, and other contributions to the local community. The vicar and the Minster continue to be actively involved in many of the town's institutions.

Text taken from the visitors' leaflet written by Tim Lamport

First World War Roll of Honour

Schooling, Cecil Herbert
Scutt, Gilbert Arthur
Seager, E.J.
Sharps, Robert

The Chaplain's Tale

Rev. Cecil Herbert Schooling

If you browse through the handwritten entries on the First World War Roll of Honour which hangs on the north wall of Croydon Minster, you will find the name of Rev. Cecil Herbert Schooling. The name does not stand out from any of the others, but what a story lays behind the simple one line entry.

This is a man, who, when he volunteered to become a Chaplain in H.M. Forces, was a curate of this church. He served St. John's, the Parish Church of Croydon, as it was called then, from 1910-1916.

Cecil was the third and youngest son of Rev. Fred Schooling and his wife Rose. Records show him being born in Wandsworth Common and the address given when he was a curate here was 2 Courtney Road, Croydon. Cecil was educated in Tonbridge School from September 1897 until 1901. After that he was educated in Germany for two years. He received both a BA and an MA from Pembroke College in Cambridge. Following training in Wells Theological College, he was made a deacon in the Church of England in 1906 and priested in 1907, serving his time at Wakefield Cathedral until 1910 when he came to Croydon. Although he does not appear on the bell ringers' list for the tower here, he must have enjoyed that aspect of church life; he was part of the Cambridge University Guild of Bellringers.

We know that he had a medical examination on 17th November 1916 to see if he was fit for the chaplaincy role for which he had volunteered. On the examination form, it states that he was 32 years old, was 72 inches tall and weighed 183 lbs. In the last box, it says that he was "fit for Military service, generally."

On the contract drawn up on 20th November 1916, it states that he was signing up for a year's service at a rate of pay of 10 shillings a day. This would be issued through Army Agents who were situated in Panton Street, Haymarket.

Rev. Schooling took part in the Battle of Messines from 7th-14th June 1917. He must have been a brave and bold man in this terrible battle as he was mentioned in despatches, printed in the London Gazette on 7th Dec 1917. At this time he was attached to the 122 Infantry Brigade. Sadly he never lived to see this citation, as he was severely wounded by a shell at Dickebusch on 20th June 1917 and died from his wounds the next day. He is buried in grave 13, Row A 21 in the military cemetery at Lijssenthoek, Poperinghe in Belgium. So Croydon lost a brave and faithful man.

The Deputy Chaplain-General wrote to his parents. "Your son was hit by a fragment from a shell that burst on the far side of the street. Seemingly no one knew that he was touched, for he stopped a lorry and clambered in. He was taken to a field ambulance about two or more miles back, and himself got out and tried to walk into the tent, when he fainted. His command over himself when so badly wounded and with his wound undressed was remarkable. There would have been no chance for him, however, even had he been dressed at once. He appears to have behaved in a most gallant manner."

A memorial service was held for Rev. Schooling, his brother and another officer, in our church on Monday 2nd July 1917. What an emotional service that would have been. We do not know what family conversations took place before he volunteered for the chaplain's role. We do not know if his brother's army service made him volunteer. What we do know is that the loss of a loved and loving curate left a hole at the very heart of this church.

Did you know?

The last Colonial Governor of Massachusetts is buried in Croydon Minster. Thomas Hutchinson was in charge of the area when tensions were running high between the colonialists and the Crown. Shortly after Thomas' official house in Boston was burned down, he left America, never to return. Living out the remainder of his life in London, he died aged 54 and was buried in the church in 1797.

The Seaman's Tale

It has been said many times that Britain is a nation of seafarers. I don't think that is so true nowadays, but wherever you live in the UK, you are never very far away from the sea, around 80 miles or so as a maximum. This tale is about a man living and working in Croydon who had a very close attachment to the sea. Alfred Herbert Hobbs was born on the 20th November 1877 in Upper Holloway. His parents were Harry and Elizabeth. Alfred was educated at the National School in Brighton. He joined the senior service, the Royal Navy, in 1895, serving aboard HMS Impregnable. He saw action in Somaliland and in the Mediterranean. After leaving the navy, he became a caretaker for the Croydon Gas Company's office. He remained a reservist and, at the commencement of the First World War, was called up. This time, he was sent to serve on HMS Cressy.

This vessel was the first of the Royal Navy fleet's armoured cruisers, built in Scotland on the Clyde, launched in 1899 and commissioned on 28th May 1901. With its four tall funnels together with masts stern and aft, Cressy had a distinctive profile.

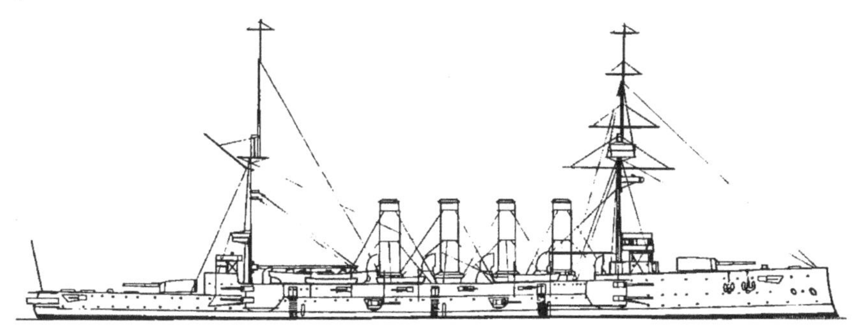

First of all, the ship was sent to serve in the China Seas. In 1907, it was transferred to the North American and West Indies Station. However, by the time of the outbreak of the First World War, it had become outdated and was virtually mothballed at its moorings in the River Medway. With the Navy needing every vessel though, the Cressy was given a thorough cleaning and overhaul. Alfred was given the rank of Leading Signalman, having been a member of the Royal Fleet Reserve and responding to the call to strengthen the senior service.

The Cressy, together with its sister ships the Aboukir and Hogue, were given the task of patrolling off the Dutch coast. The weather in the middle of September 1914 turned stormy for a couple of days and the destroyers who were meant to guard the patrol had returned to port. So it was that the three ships should have had a destroyer escort but they didn't. The three armoured cruisers should have been sailing in a zigzag fashion at 12/13 knots, but they weren't. Because of their age, the ship's commander decided to steer a straight path in order to maintain the speed required. This opened them up to attack although they had taken precautions, having posted lookouts as well as manning a gun on each side of the ship.

Unfortunately for them, U-9, a German U-boat under the command of Otto Weddigen, was sheltering from the same storm on the seabed. He was supposed to be attacking shipping in and out of the port of Ostend but when he surfaced he saw the smoke from the four funnelled ships and closed in. September 22nd 1914 would prove a fateful day. After firing torpedoes first at the Aboukir, the U-boat claimed all three ships and a total of 1,459 men lost their lives.

This number almost equals the losses on the Titanic, yet the disaster remains little known in British Naval history. The disaster was probably made worse because it was first thought that the Aboukir had struck a mine so the other two ships closed in ready to take off survivors. This resulted in the other two being easy targets for the German submariners. Of the lost sailors, 560 were from HMS Cressey.

This brief naval action changed the view of submarine warfare, with the authorities realising how important a weapon it could be.

Albert was among the huge number of fatalities on that day and his name is remembered on the Chatham Naval Memorial, plot 3. In Croydon Minster, his name is handwritten on the Croydon Roll of Honour on the north wall. He died aged 37.

Albert was married to Frances and at the outbreak of the war the couple were living at 105 Albert Road, East Croydon. Her tragedy was something she thought would not have happened. Alfred had finished his time in the Royal Navy only to lose his life when he was called up from the reservists.

Did you know?

The earliest clear record of the church's dedication to St. John the Baptist is found in the will of John de Croydon, fishmonger, dated 6th December 1347, which includes a bequest to "the church of S. John de Croydon".[3]

In its final medieval form, the church was mainly a Perpendicular-style structure of late fourteenth and early fifteenth century date. It still bears the arms of archbishops Courtenay and Chicheley, believed to have been its benefactors.

The Surgeon's Tale

When you approach the large brass plaque on the south wall of the Minster, don't make the same mistake that I did. When I read that Henry Townsend Whitling died at sea on the SS Orient, I assumed there must have been a maritime disaster and the ship went down. As I researched the tale, I soon found out how wrong was that assumption.

Henry Townsend Whitling was born in 1835. He married Emma Mary Penfold, eldest daughter of Thomas Brooks Penfold, on 28th April 1864 at Reigate Parish Church. The clergyman who officiated at the wedding was Rev. H. J. Storrs, Henry's cousin. The newspaper entry for the marriage included the information that Emma's father was formerly of the Honourable East India Company Service and was from Magill, South Australia, now a suburb of Adelaide. It was in an archived newspaper cutting of the South Australia Weekly Chronicle where the above information was discovered.

The next relevant entry for our tale in that Australian newspaper was dated 15th July 1865, when it stated that on 17th April, n Croydon, the wife of H. T. Whitling Esq., surgeon, gave birth to a daughter. This daughter was named Alice and she was christened at St. Peter's, Croydon on 28th May 1865. She was he first of eight children, seven of whom survived. Ernest, the irst born son, was given Storrs as a middle name after Henry's cousin, but didn't survive one year.

As a medical man of the town, Whitling took an interest in some of the societies and associations that flourished at this time. His name is recorded in the minutes of the Croydon Microscopical Club. In 1870 he moved the vote of thanks for the guest speaker on the evening. On another occasion, he is noted as being one of the members who had brought something to exhibit as one of their shows.

That Henry was a surgeon was an interesting fact. From the Royal College of Surgeons, we discover that in 1862 Sir James Paget, an eminent Victorian Surgeon, recommended a Henry Thomas Lanchester to Croydon as an assistant to Dr. Carpenter and Mr Whitling. That partnership between Lanchester and Whitling continued until January 1885 when it was dissolved, with a notice printed in the London Gazette. The address given for their practice was 53 High St., Croydon, with Dr. Whitling living in a house attached to the surgery. We do not know the exact reason why the practice was dissolved, but a clue could come from the reason given for Whitling sailing to Australia a few years later, namely that he had heart disease.

With the connections through his in-laws, Whitling and Emma set off on the SS Orient on a voyage to Australia where he hoped the climate would improve his health. This ship sailed regularly between England and Australia, its fastest journey time being 37 days. It was built on the Clyde by John Elder and Co. in 1879 and was then the biggest ever Clyde-built ship. The Orient name lives on today through the Leyton Orient Football Club, founded as they were by an employee who was keen to keep the "Orient" name alive.

Unfortunately, Whitling's heart disease was greatly accelerated by unusual and intensely hot weather on the voyage and he died while the ship was still in the Indian Ocean. His death was recorded when the Orient docked in Adelaide.

The British Medical Journal wrote on 25th May 1889: "He was very dearly loved by his wife, seven children, relations and a very large circle of friends. He was deservedly respected and esteemed by everyone who knew him."

The SS Orient

Did you know?

One of the greatest American portrait painters of the eighteenth century is buried in Croydon Minster. John Singleton Copley was born in Boston and quickly gained a huge reputation, painting many society portraits. He embarked on a European Tour to enhance and expand his skills. Because of the American War of Independence, he never returned to America. His son became Lord Lyndhurst and served as Chancellor of the Exchequer three times. Copley died in 1815.

A Troubled Tale

How would you feel if the vicar of this church was arrested, charged and found guilty of an offence at the Old Bailey? What would the congregation say when they heard that their vicar had been held up by a highwayman? How would ordinary church folk go about getting rid of their vicar who wasn't doing his job properly?

If you could go back to the seventeenth century, you could find answers to these questions right here in this church. As you enter the building and look left at the board which shows the list of vicars over the years, you'll see the name of William Clewer, 1666-1684. Behind his name there lies a raft of stories, scandals, arrests and court appearances which shocked not only Croydon, but London, too.

Rev. William Clewer was made vicar here in October 1660 by Archbishop Juxom at the recommendation of Charles II who "had been imposed upon with regard to his character". This, in itself, is quite strange as Clewer spent the years of the Commonwealth chiding and deriding members of the Royalist cause. Following the demise of Cromwell, Clewer made speedy representations to the Earl of Cleveden asking him for a "good" parish. St. John's Croydon fitted that bill.

William was born in 1628, the son of William, as was usually the case in those days with the firstborn son being named after his father. The family lived in Towcester, Northamptonshire. He went up to Christ's College, Cambridge at the age of 15. He received his BA in 1646 and his MA in 1650. Nothing here, it would seem, that would change his later outlook on life.

By this time, in conjunction with his studying, he was made rector of Ashton, Northants being at that time just 18 years old but "of a very ill life and very troublesome to his neighbours" wrote one observer. This is the first negative reference that we find about him. He was married to Elizabeth. She died and was buried on 25th November 1671, in Lady Scudamore's grave, in the middle chancel of the church here. It was in that same year that he was awarded his Doctorate of Divinty from Cambridge.

Things certainly took a downward turn in the years he spent at Croydon. From evidence given in court, we can see that he wasn't a very conscientious clergyman. We do know he carried out some duties as a vicar. In our parish records, it states that William, son of William Merredew, was baptised by Clewer in 1672. However, by that time, he had already been taken to ecclesiastical court for neglect of duties, getting off with a "monishment". Two further court appearances in 1681 and 1682 followed for neglect of duties. Initially he received a suspension which was subsequently overturned and a further monishment.

In 1684, he was finally deprived of his living and removed from his perpetual vicar's post here. The case, brought by the Inhabitants of Croydon, and fronted by a parishioner O.J.Pullen, is a famous one. Because of Clewer's appeals, the case had dragged on and on taking over 10 years for the court to reach the decision which the parishioners wanted.

He was accused of many things in his lifetime, including drunkenness and keeping a mistress. He was tried and convicted at the Old Bailey for stealing a silver cup. His punishment was to be burnt on the hand.

In December 1690, he again appeared at the Old Bailey accused with others of kidnapping and then forcibly marrying a young heiress to her "suitor". The girl was Mary Wharton and she was 14 at the time. Clewer, in his defence, claimed he knew nothing about abductions and just performed a wedding ceremony in a guesthouse in Westminster where he was lodging. He was acquitted of the offence, although another man was found guilty of kidnap. Mary had been taken from outside her home where she lived with her mother and forced to marry Captain James Campbell. The marriage was later annulled by an Act of Parliament. The Honourable James Campbell later went on to serve an a member of the House of Commons.

In a book, *The Lives of Highwaymen*, there is a passage stating that Clewer was held up by a notorious highwayman, O'Brien, in Acton. Clewer, who allegedly knew the rogue, said his money was safe back home in Croydon. He produced a deck of cards and asked O'Brien to play a game of All Fours with his canonicals as the prize, as he had no money with him. Clewer lost and walked home in his shirt!

Clewer died in 1702. The note in St. Bride's Church register in London calls him "parson of Croydon." There seemed to be no end to accusations against him. In this brief outline, I will leave you with one more; in court, he was accused of reading out sermons published by other clerics and claiming them for his own. He obviously ran out of preparation time!

Did you know?

Dorinda Nelligan, who has a plaque to commemorate her life in the church, was in one of the earliest group of nurses to serve in the Red Cross, tending to the sick and wounded in the Franco-Prussian War in 1870-71. Later, she became the first Headmistress of Croydon High School.

The Curate's Tale

A church curate should never be surprised by any task which their vicar asks them to do. I suspect that statement to be as true down the ages as it is today. It is just that the actual jobs may have changed. Back in 1550, the curate of our church was John Goodwyn. On 19th March of that year, his task was clear and straightforward. He had to make an inventory of everything that was in the church. This sounds a straightforward job, but where would you start? If you were charged with such a task today, how would you organise it? What would be first on your list?

Curate John had the two churchwardens, Hugh Davy and John a-Wood of Addyscoom, to assist him in the task. I have used the original spellings here, as written out in the inventory so you can see how the record was begun. The year 1550 was described by the clerk as the third year of the reign of Edward VI.

Our Tudor listmakers had to decide what would come first. I suspect you may not have chosen the church bells to be at the beginning of the document but this is what was written down then. The complete first entry read, "Item first v belles and a lytle sanctes bell." We are not given the size of the five bells but we can assume that the little sanctuary bell was smaller and similar to today's tolling bell.

Precious objects would be to the front of their minds as well as ours, I suspect, in listing what is in the church. There is little surprise, then, that the next entry reads, "Item a crosse of sylver and gylte with an ymage on every side and the crucifix in the mydes." This then would probably be the cross which stood on the altar.

Many items were presented to the church then, just as they are now, in memory of a loved one. Some were gifts for no other reason that the church played a major part in their lives and they wished to acknowledge the fact. Central to the worship of this church today is the Eucharist, as would have been in Tudor times. The third entry for the inventory reads, "A cuppe of sylver and gilte to bere the sacrament in of the gyfte of William Warr." There were several items which follow this one which gave the details of various communion sets of a chalice, the cup, and a paten, a small plate for the wafer. Item 5 reads, "Another chalice parcel gylte with a crucifix in the fote and the paten with a Sen Johan's hede in the mides thereof." St. John's head being important to link with the saint to whom this church is dedicated.

One other entry in this part of the inventory stands out. We wouldn't really think of the church lending items such as a chalice or paten but the wording of this entry is quite definite. "Iteme a challyce which was lent unto Mr Thomas Heron the whych ye kept frome the churche untyll this day." From the strength of this sentence, one can imagine the curate, or indeed the vicar, reminding Thomas to return the chalice to the church as they are making an inventory and they need it back. Thomas Heron was a wealthy man of the day, living in Addiscombe House, Shirley Road.

Thomas died in 1518. There was a large family tomb destroyed in the church fire of 1867. One of the brasses on the choir wall today commemorates Thomas' son William, who was a distinguished Justice of the Peace for Surrey.

The chalice and the paten would not have stood on plain wood and so the inventory included the cloths upon which they would have stood. The first entry about the altar cloths is a stunning one. "Item two aulter clothes to the high aulter for above and benethe of damask and satten at the gyfte of the Frenshe Queene." So that any uncertainty may be removed from your mind, the French Queen referred to is Mary Tudor. Mary and her brother Henry would have been well acquainted with Croydon through the Archbishop's Palace. Mary became the third wife of Louis 12th of France, she being 18 years old and him 52. He died only three months after their wedding, and Mary went on to marry the Earl of Suffolk, Charles Brandon. She died in 1533, several years before this inventory was taken, and so one can imagine the feeling that people would have had for this gift from the royal lady who was known as the Queen of France by many for the rest of her life.

Two other gifts of altar cloths stand out. One which "was set abowte with perls and of nedleworke" was the gift of mystrys Morely." The other is an alter cloth of green, "brodred with flowers at the gift of Elys Davys," the man whose endowments resulted in the building of the Elys Davy Almshouses.

If you have been making a mental note of all the items that need to be listed in the church, I hope you have written down the priests' vestments. Of these, there were many and again several were the gifts from parishioners. Mystres Redynge gave "a hole suet of vestments priest decon and subdeacon of satten brodred with letters of golde with abes and the apparel thereto." They must have looked impressive, as indeed they should, having been given by such a lady. The Redynge family were very much part of the Tudor aristocracy. Mystres Mary Redynge was Mistress to the Prince of Castell and was married to John Redynge who was part of King Henry VIII's entourage when he was young. John died in 1508. Mary Redynge was the daughter of Sir William Brandon and was the aunt of the Earl of Suffolk who married Mary Tudor, already mentioned as presenting a gift to this church.

There is another set of vestments included which were the gift of "Lord Moreton". Archbishop Morton held the seat at Canterbury in 1486-1500 spending a great deal of his time at the Archbishop's Palace here in Croydon.

When you have read through 54 entries of the inventory, you eventually come to the line which reads, "Item a Byble." I wonder why it was so low down on the list? It is also strange to us who have so many Bibles that we forget, sometimes, that most churches in those days would have just one. Only one other book is mentioned in the inventory, that one being the sayings of Eramus.

Almost at the end of the inventory, there is one final noteworthy line which I shall include in this tale. It is that the church had "a payre of organes." I will leave to the Tudor musicologists exactly what they would have looked like, but it is good to know that even in the middle of the sixteenth century, music was important in this church, just as it is now. However, I don't think I would have wanted the job of hand pumping the bellows to ensure a proper sound.

I hope Curate John had a sense of achievement in completing his task. I suspect he would be flabbergasted to know that people could gain much interest from it by reading it over 400 years later.

Did you know?

Edmund Grindal was the Archbishop of Canterbury from 1575 until his death in 1583. His tomb in Croydon Minster was destroyed by the fire in 1867. A plaque marks the spot today. In Edmund Spencer's famous poem of the day, *The Shepherd's Calendar,* Grindal is mentioned by way of an anagram, Old Algrind. After he died, John Whitgift was appointed as the new Archbishop.

The Churchwarden's Tale

When I came across Knevit Leppingwell while conducting some recent research, I immediately stopped my study in order to focus on this very interesting and striking name. If you have ever carried out research on family history, then you will know that some names stand out from those around them. This one certainly did and what I discovered is now constructed into the churchwarden's tale.

Mr Leppingwell was the churchwarden of Croydon Parish Church in 1817, together with a Mr Thomas Hewson. The churchwardens were very important in the life of an Anglican Church, just as they are today. Looking through our church records, you will find several examples of what a pair of churchwardens managed to achieve during their time of tenure. William Inkpen, the principal coach proprietor of the time in Croydon, and John Brooker, who were churchwardens in 1829, oversaw the completion of a new window on the north wall of the building. James Rogers and Francis Symmonds were credited with repairing the St. Nicholas Chapel in 1815, in particular with "Roman cement".

In a noted Croydon historical book, we can find out exactly what Mr Leppingwell and Mr Hewson were involved with in their church duties.

We read that, "In this present year 1817 considerable alterations and improvements have been made both in the interior and exterior of this handsome gothic edifice. The wall at the east end of the St. Mary's Chantry and the vestry room which was in a delapsed state have been effectually repaired with cement, and the fine gothic window therein restored to its original order above which is the following description. This chancel end repaired Knevit Leppingwell and Thomas Hewson, churchwardens 1817."

Unfortunately, because of the fire which was to destroy most of the church building in 1869, nothing remains of the improvements which were achieved in 1817, except this record in an historic publication.

But what of Knevit and his personal life? In the 1841 census, we can discover that he was 63 years old. This would place his year of birth either in 1777 or 1778. This fits with what is recorded at St. Nicholas Church, Castle Hedingham in Essex, where it states that Knevit was baptised on 6th July 1778. He was given the name Knevit as it is his mother's maiden name. She was Jane Louisa Knevit who married his father John on 9th June 1772.

The couple had six children in total. From this information, we can thus calculate that Knevit would have been churchwarden at the age of 40. He was living at 710 High Street, Croydon at the time of the 1841 census and was married to Caroline Biggs. They had a daughter, Emma Annette, who was born in 1817. We next find his name on the list of Governors and Officers of the Asylum for the support and education of deaf and dumb children published in 1821. Here he is noted as K.L. Esq. Croydon.

In order for Knevit to be on this list, he would have had to pay "not less than 10 guineas to become a governor for life". If one donated more money, then you got an additional vote at meetings for every additional 50 guineas donated. The sum of £200 guaranteed you one child's place for life. The establishment, based in Old Kent Road, London was set up for 200 children. A search through the names of children residing there in 1821, though, revealed no surname link to our churchwarden.

In 1822, however, his life and his family's life were dealt a hammer blow. On 16th March, Knevit Leppingwell, linen draper, was declared bankrupt. You can see his name almost at the bottom of this list, which was published in the Edinburgh Gazette of the time. What exactly that meant in his day-to-day life we do not know, we can only speculate.

We can deduce, though, that Knevit did not let the bankruptcy affect him for the remainder of his life. We have already found out that he was living in the High Street in 1841 and when his will was proven on 20th October 1849, it states that he was a "gentleman of Croydon". He must have regained his social standing in the town. He passed away on 21st September that year, aged 72, and was buried in the churchyard here. His grave was on the south side of the church but was one of the many where the headstone was removed and the remains reinterred when the graveyard was altered years later.

The tomb of Archbishop Sheldon

The Boer War Tale

Private Clarence Snelling (service number 7554) is remembered on a brass plaque on the north wall of our church. The memorial was bought and erected by the Officers, NCOs and Privates of the 2nd Volunteer Service Company of The Queen's Royal West Surrey Regiment. Clarence was a casualty of the Boer War in South Africa. This was a conflict at the end of the nineteenth and the early twentieth century in which 7,500 British soldiers were either killed in action or died of wounds, while almost twice as many, 13,000, died of disease. Clarence was one of those of the latter category, dying of enteric fever which today we would call typhoid. Clarence died on 30th April 1902.

As well as being remembered in Croydon, Clarence's name can be found on the Roll of Honour in the Kroonstad Garden of Remembrance, near to where he died. You can see his name at the end of the list of the 21 men of the Royal West Surrey Regiment, their names etched into a black marble stone, who are buried there. As well as the Royal West Kent, other soldiers and auxiliaries from the East Kent Regiment (The Buffs) and Royal Engineers are remembered on this Roll of Honour. These men who lost their lives in South Africa were originally buried in a number of different, smaller cemeteries but were reinterred later in Kroonstad.

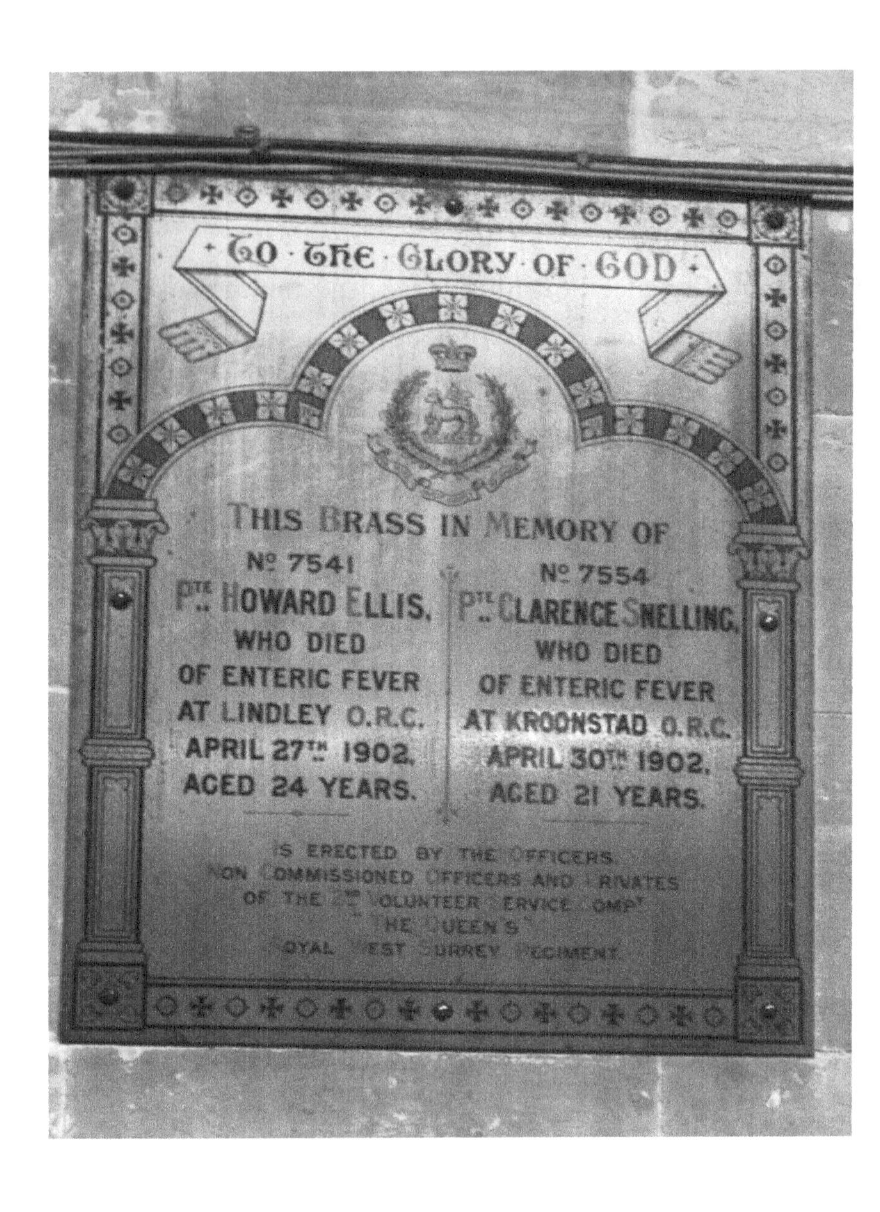

Kroonstad is Afrikaans for Crown City. The initials, ORC, which can be seen on the Minster plaque after the town name, stand for Orange River Colony. This was the British colony created after Britain first occupied, in 1900, then annexed, in 1902, the Orange Free State in the second Boer War.

The colony ceased to exist in 1910 when it was absorbed into the Union of South Africa as Orange Free State Province. Kroonstad was the site of one of the camps which the British set up to imprison many of the Boers.

Clarence, who was a volunteer, signed up to serve his country but never returned, leaving a family to mourn his loss. He was born in Tooting, possibly at the hospital, the eldest child of Frederick and Caroline Snelling.

They were married on 2nd August 1875 at Holy Trinity Church, Wimbledon. His siblings were Harry, Edgar, Edith and Eva. Their father was a baker and in 1901 the family were living at 126 Cherry Orchard Road, Croydon. The 1891 census tells us that they were then living at 266 Dartnell Road, Croydon. Before that, the family were living in Tunbridge Wells, the 1881 address given as 18 High Street. In 1881, Clarence's father is described as a head baker, whereas in 1901 he is a bread maker. Was this a promotion or a more specialised position?

The immediate Snelling family had connections to Croydon for a long time as his brother Harry passed away here in the town, at the age of 75, in April 1962.

On the plaque in the Minster, another volunteer from Croydon, Howard Ellis, is also remembered. A short walk down the church towards the lady chapel will reveal that there is another small memorial to a soldier in the Boer War. Here you can find that a third Croydon resident, Private James Laver, of the Royal Lancers, was also a casualty, being killed in action on 14th July 1901.

The Tale of Pat McCormick

What else could you possibly add to a person's CV which contains being a missionary, a Chaplain in HM Forces, a Canon of Canterbury Cathedral and a familiar name on radio broadcast services? What about adding in a DSO for being mentioned in despatches four times? What about playing in a first class cricket match, representing the MCC in 1907? What about playing rugby for the Transvaal? Anything else to add? There is, of course, one more thing; being the vicar of Croydon.

If you look down the list of vicars displayed on the board at the entrance of the Minster, you will see the name of William Patrick McCormick, who was vicar here just after the Great War from 1919-1927. His tale is a fascinating one. His life was full and eventful, and he touched the hearts, minds and souls of hundreds and thousands of people.

Born in Hull in 1877, his father was Rev. Joseph McCormick, later the vicar of St. James, Piccadilly and his mother was Frances, the daughter of Lt. Colonel with the East India Company. Pat, as he was to be known, went up to St. John's College, Cambridge where he gained a BA in 1899. He received his MA later in 1907. After teaching for a year, he was ordained deacon in Rochester in 1901 and priested the following year.

Straightaway he obtained a temporary chaplaincy role in the forces that were fighting at the very end of the Boer War and so he left for South Africa. Rather than returning home at the end of the war, he saw a real need to further God's work in the Rand district. He ministered among the mining communities, living in the accommodation provided for them at the Jumpers Deep (Gold) Mine.

Quickly gaining the miners' respect, his sporting prowess in rugby and cricket was admired by all. The recognition of his rugby prowess came in South Africa when he represented the Transvaal in the Currie Cup at rugby both in 1904 and in 1906. In those days, the Currie Cup was not played annually. For each competition, he played three times for Transvaal. In 1904, they played Free State, Borders and North East Districts, all played in East London. In 1906, they played Free State, Border and Eastern Province, this time in Johannesburg. Rev. Pat played club rugby for the Wanderers, one of the oldest rugby teams in South Africa which was based in Johannesburg.

He played for them in 1903 when the club got a team together again after the Boer War and helped them to lift the Grand Challenge Cup that year. He had a good sporting pedigree as his father rowed for Cambridge in 1856 and was also an excellent cricketer and boxer! The parish of St. Patrick, Cleveland, Transvaal was established through Pat's endeavours. The church was built, services and routines developed, and he ministered there until 1910 when he was appointed to the vicar's job at St. John's, Belgravia, in Johannesburg. He stayed for four years, meeting and marrying his wife Miriam there.

Returning to the UK in 1914, he responded again to the Chaplaincy call. He crossed the Channel in August 1914 on the SS Italian Prince where he was recorded as Temporary Chaplain to HM Forces, 4th class. He may have started at the bottom of the chaplaincy group but the London Gazette of 28th October 1918 recorded that Rev. McCormick was to be made Chaplain 1st class with the pay and allowances of that rank. He was involved in the conflict straightaway back in September 1914, taking ambulances from Nantes to the BEF HQ at Fere-en-Tardenois in Picardy. Indeed, it's largely through his efforts of persuasion that more motor ambulances were assigned to the British Expeditionary Force.

As chaplain to the RAMC No 1 Motor Ambulance Convoy based on St. Omer and Poperinghe, he was heavily involved in the evacuation of wounded from Ypres during the 1st Battle of Ypres (October 1914 - January 1915). Amongst many ventures and tasks assigned to him during the war, it is notable that he organised a soldiers' club at St. Omer, got concert parties to entertain the troops at Le Havre, and arranged cinema screenings in Poperinghe.

Being chaplain to the 3rd Guards Brigade (Guards Division) included service in the Battle of Loos (September - November 1915). This also brought him into contact with HRH the Prince of Wales and other prominent figures in the Guards Battalion. In a biography about the most well-known of all First World War chaplains "Woodbine Willie", the Rev. Studdert Kennedy, it states that Rev. Pat had visited him both in France and at home in England, and was much inspired by Rev. Stuttert Kennedy's preaching and ministry.

Patrick served notably with HM Forces being twice mentioned in despatches, firstly on 30th November 1915 and secondly on 13th November 1916. He was subsequently awarded a DSO on 1st January 1917.

St Martins-in-the-Fields

In 1927, Pat was appointed to the post of vicar of St. Martin's-in-the-Fields near Trafalgar Square. He gained this position following the retirement of Rev. Dick Sheppard who was well known for his work with "down and outs". Rev. Pat continued and developed this special ministry. During the 1930s, his voice became well known over the airwaves as many services on the Home Service were broadcast from St. Martin-in-the-Fields. His appointment as chaplain to the King meant that he then got to know members of the Royal family, taking services for them at St. Georges in Windsor.

Rev. Pat suffered periods of ill health in the late 1930s and was away from his work because of the heart problems which were to cause his death very suddenly in October 1940. The daily routines of the church had been made much more complex because of the Blitz by the German Luftwaffe. The crypt at St. Martins was pressed into service as a nightly air raid shelter and many felt that the strain of this situation contributed to his fatal heart attack.

In the telling of this tale, I almost forgot to say that he was vicar of Croydon from 1919-1927. Judging by what he achieved throughout all the other phases of his life, I reckon it was a fruitful time too, but that is the subject for another story.

The Tudor Tale

Life in Tudor times for a priest would have been difficult. Henry VIII's break with Rome, together with the beginning of the Reformation, meant that priests had to take sides. That proved to a life-changing decision for many.

The tale which is outlined here concerns the vicar of Croydon Parish Church at the time of Henry's reign, one Rev. Dr. Roland Phillips. He was collated into the church here on 4th June 1497 by Archbishop Morton. This collation was agreed unanimously by the prior and convent of St. Saviour's Bermondsey, to whom this church was linked in those days. He retired on 9th May 1538. We know that in retirement he was awarded a pension of 12 pounds a year, "to be taken from the profits of the vicarage". The pension was issued by a decree from Archbishop Thomas

Cranmer through his vicar-general at the time, John Cocke. Phillips was given this "due to his great age".

During his time at Croydon, Rev. Dr. Phillips was never afraid to speak his mind. Indeed, his orthodox views and his devotion to Catholicism got him noticed by the very highest authorities in the land. Thomas More, the Lord Chancellor who eventually was beheaded for his refusal to acknowledge Anne as the new Queen, wrote in his diary that he was brought before the Lords at Lambeth Palace in 1534 to swear the oath of allegiance: "When I was before the Lords at Lambeth I was the first to be called in, albeit that Mast. Doc, vicar of Croydon, came before me and divers others." More went on, "I heard the Master Doctor (Vicar of Croydon) and all the remnants of the priests in London who were sent for were sworn." Roland Phillips was persuaded to change his mind and sign the document.

It can be seen from other sources that Roland Phillips was a follower of More's thinking and writing. In the introductory letter to his book *Utopia*, More wrote to his friend Peter Giles from Antwerp. Giles was asked if he would enquire from the ancient mariner where Utopia was, because he had a learned and pious man who was keen to go and be the first missionary to the pagans. It was widely thought that Roland Phillips was that learned and pious individual.

Archbishop Thomas Cranmer was one whose attention was drawn by the Vicar of Croydon's outspoken views. Sources state that on more than one occasion, Phillips was imprisoned by Cranmer who "often resided in Croydon" and who presumably heard first hand reports of him speaking out in favour of Rome. Being brought before the Archbishop's court in July 1536, Phillips was interrogated for speaking out against Royal policy.

The previous summer, Phillips had been used by Cromwell, on the advice of John Walley, to try persuade the Carthusians to renounce their popish ways through his preaching. Throughout his priesthood, he was known for his powerful oratory. Phillips preached at many notable services, including at the funeral of Abbot Islip in 1532 who was the abbot of the monastery at Westminster. He wasn't keen on new ways though.

As a Canon of St. Paul's Cathedral, he famously spoke out once about the new printing presses: "We (the Church) must root out printing or printing will root us out." Times change!

During his questioning in the Archbishop's court in 1536, Phillips was asked about his view of the bread and the wine. He was also quizzed about worshipping God as spirit. If this were true, said his inquisitors, then there would be no need to pray out loud. Phillips told the court he knew of no one who kept a silence in the Mass. Just two years after his trial, Rev. Dr. Roland Phillips retired.

As well as serving as vicar of Croydon, he was also appointed as warden of Merton College, Oxford from 1521-25. Holinshed, writing in his chronicles first published in 1577, described Phillips as "esteemed" and as "a noble preacher". His Tudor tale was certainly a colourful one. One can reflect that Phillips did well to last so long in life, treading a precarious path while others around him lost their lives in the religious strife of the age.

The Translator's Tale

This is a tale of someone who, in all probability, only ever came into the Croydon Church building on one occasion. The date of that visit was 20th July 1595. It was a Thursday.

The reason for the visit was that the individual concerned was to be consecrated, in a service led by John Whigift the Archbishop of Canterbury, to the Bishop's seat at Llandaff in Wales. Also officiating at that service was Richard, Bishop of London; William, Bishop of Norwich; and John, Bishop of Rochester. The individual concerned was the Rev. William Morgan. This service says much about the importance of Croydon in those days, particularly in relation to church history, because Whitgift spent a lot of time at his Palace and much important business was completed here.

Other bishops consecrations were held in Croydon, but sometimes it is recorded that they were held in Croydon Chapel, which would have been a part of the Palace. William Morgan, though, was made bishop here, as it says, "in Croydon Church."

It would have been a long journey for William and his wife Catherine to travel from their home in Wales to Croydon. At the time, they were living in the vicarage of Llanrhaeadr-ym-Mochnant.

One may think it a surprise that a vicar from a small parish about forty miles north west of the town of Welshpool should be standing here in Croydon Parish Church, as it was then, in front of the Archbishop, but William and John Whitgift's paths would have crossed earlier in their lives. They would have been acquainted with each other from their days at Cambridge University. A look at William's earlier life helps to put his visit to Croydon in context.

William was born in a house called Ty Mawr, at Wybrnant in the parish of Penmachno. The house overlooks the River Conwy. Today it is owned by the National Trust and has much information and many artefacts on display about the life of William Morgan. Although the date is disputed by some, he was probably born in the year 1545. His parents were John ap Morgan and Lowri. John was a copyhold tenant on the estate of the Wynn family of Gwydir Castle near Llanrwst. It was a tradition that the Wynn family would invite the brightest children of local families to be educated at their house and at their expense. In this environment, William began his lifelong love of the Welsh language and literature. William was very lucky to be boarded with a family who knew the value of education and, in particular, a university education.

There was an uncle of the Wynn family who was a professor at Cambridge. William went up to that university when he was about 20. Although this seems quite late in his life, it was not uncommon in those days. In order to help support his time at St. John's, William would have been a sort of servant-cum-valet to wealthy students. The term sizer describes this role and records show that William moved from being a sub-sizer to a proper sizer after a couple of years. These additional duties, though, did not prevent him from studying hard. William was at Cambridge from 1565 to 1571.

After gaining his Bachelor of Arts degree in 1568, William was ordained deacon at Ely Cathedral. At this time, he embarked on his MA studies. He learned Hebrew under Antoine Chevallier, who had been Elizabeth I's French tutor but who had to flee to Germany under Mary's reign. It very probable that William picked up some French from this tutor but it is his brilliance in Hebrew that was to set him apart from most others of his day.

In 1572, he was appointed the vicar in the parish of Llanbadarn Fawr near Aberystwyth. After three years there, he was appointed as the vicar of Welshpool, thanks to the influence of his friend William Hughes who was the Bishop of St. Asaph's.

It was while he was at Welshpool that he was given three other parishes, appointing a deputy who took services for him. This gave William the time, and more money, so that he could carry on with his studies. However it was his move to Llanrhaeadr-ym-Mochnant in 1578, staying there until his appointment to Llandaff, where he made his name. Using his excellent knowledge of Hebrew, coupled with his supreme understanding of Welsh Literature and poetry, he became the first person to translate the whole of the Bible into Welsh. He completed this huge task in 1588. In fact, for a whole year previously, William had lived in London, adjacent to the printers who needed very close attention by the author so that his Welsh translation was absolutely correct. Although it is speculation, it is probable that Whitgift and Morgan became further acquainted as the Welsh Bible was being readied for print.

When speaking with some of my Welsh friends about the fact that Whitgift was buried in Croydon, they immediately spoke about their understanding of his influence in getting the Bible translated into Welsh. Thus we have in the service of consecration not only the driver of the project but also the completer. June 20th 1595 was not only an important day in Croydon, it was important for Wales.

William and his wife returned to South Wales, this time living very close to the cathedral at Llandaff. William continued his translations, revising the edition of the New Testament and translating the Book of Common Prayer, which was published in 1599.

After his friend William Hughes died, our William was appointed to the Bishop's seat at St. Asaph. John Whigift was again influential in the appointment which doubled William's salary as he was appointed as the Archdeacon as well as the Bishop! He and his wife lived in the Archdeacon's house in Dyseth for the rest of his life. William died in September 1604. He was buried in St. Asaph's near the High Altar, although there is no memorial stone to mark the spot. Catherine lived for another year, having moved back to Oswestry where her family had originated. A copy of William Morgan's Bible can be seen today on display in St. Asaph's Cathedral.

William's will shows that he was certainly not a rich man when he died, even though in his latter years he paid for the re-roofing of the cathedral from his own purse. The value of the goods he left totalled £110. Among the collection were 45 pewter vessels, five flower pots, two peacocks and two swans. Other household items named included "a curten over the doore, a looking glasse and a payre of sheets". William lived frugally in great contrast to the Tudor gentry who supported his education and, indeed, to the Archbishop who consecrated him in Croydon. His legacy, though, is huge. His Welsh translation of the Bible was one of the most significant literary and ecclesiastical achievements, not only for his time, but for generations to come. His consecration in Croydon provided him with the platform for fame, but not riches. And I believe that was what he would have wanted.

The only visible link about this tale to be found in Croydon Minster today is in the stained glass window above Whitgift's tomb in the St. Nicholas Chapel, where you can see a crest in the bottom right hand corner with the wording, "principality of Wales."

THOMAS BUCHNER. D.D.
SAMUEL OTES. M.A.
FRANCIS PECK.
EDWARD CORBETT. M.A.
JONATHAN WESTWOOD.
WILLIAM CLEWER. D.D. 1660
HENRY HUGHES. M.A.
JOHN CÆSAR. M.A.
ANDREW TREBECK. B.D. 1720.
NATHANIEL COLLIER. M.A. 1727.
JOHN VADE. M.A.
EAST APTHORP. D.D. 1765.
JOHN IRELAND. D.D.
J.C. LOCKWOOD. M.A. 1816.

The Tale of Rev. John Vade

If you stop just inside the entrance doors of Croydon Minster, turn left and look at the list of vicars of the church, you can read a great long line of people who have held this post over hundreds of years. This tale is about Rev. John Vade, whose name you can find on the brass plaque, and who was vicar here until his death in 1765. His passing was surely an untimely one as he was aged just 42. He left behind a wife, Elizabeth, and two children, Mary and Ashton. He, his wife, and their daughter Mary, who died in 1790, were buried here but their tomb was destroyed in the church fire of 1869. His wife Elizabeth, who died in 1800 aged 80, came from Rochester. This is an important piece of information as quite a bit of our tale is found in the county of Kent.

John was born in Bromley, Kent, the son of William Vade, an apothecary. During the eighteenth century, medical licenses to practise medicine and surgery were issued by the Archbishop of Canterbury in his Diocese and records show that William was granted his license in 1716. As it happened, the Archbishop of Canterbury issuing that license was William Wake, who also had his tomb here in Croydon after his death.

John went up to Clare College, Cambridge and received his BA degree in 1744, followed by his MA three years later. He was ordained deacon in Rochester Cathedral in 1744 and priested in 1746. This led to a move to Cambridgeshire where he became vicar of Isleham from 1746 to 1751, this parish coming under the jurisdiction of Rochester. His ecclesiastical career took him back to Kent to the church of St. Nicholas with St. Clement in Rochester as vicar. He was next appointed vicar of Croydon in 1755, holding both positions until his death, as well as being chaplain to the Bishop of Rochester. Holding a dual role as vicar was not uncommon in those days and a curate was appointed to do much of the day-to-day work as well as to lead the services. *The Gentlemen's Magazine* from 1755 noted that a Dispensation for Rev. Vade to hold two livings had been granted, with a salary of £350 per year.

John married a woman named Elizabeth Wharam. She is described in one source as "being the daughter and sole heiress of David Wharam, Rochester". When you read the word heiress, it makes you think that there must be some money or property connected to this family. A search for her father reveals that he was a very important figure in the town, reaching the position of Alderman. He was appointed Mayor of Rochester in 1744.

The Vade family had some interesting connections. In an unusual will, proved in August 1749, of Lieutenant Samuel Crouchman, Elizabeth was bequeathed a diamond gold mourning ring and her father a gold beaded cane. It is not clear how the Wharams were linked to First Lieutenant Crouchman of the Marines. We do know, though, that the naval officer was executed for mutiny, because of what happened at Cape-Coast Africa when he tried to sail off in the King's vessel. Following a court martial when they returned to this country, he was shot at Portsmouth.

John's father, in his role of apothecary, visited many well-to-do folk, one of whom was Sir John Leigh, who lived in nearby Addington. Sir John saw all his three children die before adulthood, as well as losing his wife Elizabeth back in 1707. Mr Douglas, a London surgeon, persuaded William Vade to take part in a plan to marry Sir John off to Vade's own daughter Elizabeth. Vade objected at first at the notion of a teenage girl being married to a 55-year-old who was certainly in poor health. However, the wedding eventually took place at Longacre at midnight on 16th May 1733 and is recorded in the Fleet Registers for legal but clandestine marriages. Later in the Court of Chancery, it was claimed by other members of the Leigh family that William Vade had complete hold over Sir John. They maintained the marriage ceremony went ahead with Sir John propped up on cushions and too ill, or drunk, to speak. The marriage, though, did not last for long as Elizabeth died in 1736. After Sir John died, the following year, the courts eventually decided that his estates in Middlesex and Kent were to be settled to William Vade in fee for his medical practices. The rest of the estate was to be given to his heirs in law.

Quite how our John Vade reacted to this family saga, we do not know. He was still quite young at this point. We can only speculate on the situation, as indeed did many people at the time! Looking into John and Elizabeth's family, we find their son, Ashton, followed his father firstly to Cambridge where he studied at Jesus College and then into the church, becoming curate locally in Chaldon, and later chaplain to the then Prince of Wales in 1792. Ashton married Rachel, the daughter of Richard Walpole, MP for Great Yarmouth and younger brother of Sir

Robert, the then Prime Minister. It seems that the Vade family couldn't stop themselves from being attracted to the nobility of the land. If only our John could have lived longer, then perhaps he would have risen further in the ecclesiastical ranks...

The Mustard Maker's Tale

I wonder how many times a member of the clergy has stood in the pulpit of Croydon Minster and spoken on the parable of the mustard seed? As they spoke to the congregation, looking into the light coming through the window over the west door, they probably would not have realised that this window is dedicated to Thomas Keen. He was a great Victorian benefactor of Croydon and was a major producer of mustard. This window of plain glass was put in the church and dedicated to Thomas after his death in 1862, at the age of 61.

So who was this man of mustard? Thomas Keen was born in Camberwell in 1801, and was heir to the Keen family business, which was the first mustard factory to be opened in London.

Their premises were in Garlick Hill, very close to the Mansion Tube station of today, and were opened in 1742. It was not until the 1720s that mustard had appeared on English tables. This condiment was first made by Mrs Clements of Durham, and was therefore known as 'Durham Mustard'. When George I became one of its devotees, nobody would eat beef without mustard.

The Keen family manufactured other spices (including curry powder, exported to Australia from the 1840s), and oatmeal and ground rice, and made their own tins, filled in the 'penny packing room'. Another product was Oxford Bleu for laundry, which stained everything, including the workers, so was done in a sealed area of the factory. The firm is linked with the term "as keen as mustard" although the phrase had appeared in print before the setting up of their factory.

The family subsequently moved to Croydon, and ran the 311-acre Welcomes Farm in Coulsdon. In 1825, Thomas married Harriett Toulmin, whose family lived at The Elms, 61 High Street, and the couple moved in there in 1831.

This house, built about 1794, was set in a two-acre garden and had a steep drive leading down to the High Street. It was flanked by two breweries, Nalder & Collyer and Crowleys. Nevertheless in a little book published in 1849, entitled *The Beauties of Surrey*, the garden of The Elms is described with about 120 other seats of the nobility and gentry.

Thomas was a great benefactor to the whole community. It was said of him that in him, "the 'unbefriended' found a friend, the sorrowful a comforter and the necessitous a generous helper." In 1857, the first Croydon church with free pews was built, St Andrews-Chapel-at-Ease, on land Thomas gave in Southbridge Meadows. In 1861, it became St. Andrew's Parish Church which today can be described as being near the flyover.

A year later, he died, on 17th February 1862, at the age of 61. *The Croydon Chronicle* reported of the funeral at Norwood Cemetery "...the arrangements for the funeral of Mr Keen were for those of an English Gentleman.

“The general closing of the shops during the passage of the procession through the town was a spontaneous tribute to a good man’s worth. His benefactions have now ceased.”

Thomas Keen is remembered with the naming of Keens Road on his former Southbridge Meadows near to St. Andrews Church. In 1862, the year Thomas died, the business changed. Keens amalgamated with Robinson & Belville, founded in 1823, who were manufacturers of patented groats and barley. We are very familiar with their ‘barley water’. Later in 1903, this new business was acquired by Colman’s, who were based in Norwich, the name we associate with mustard today.

The seeds that Thomas sewed in his business life certainly grew well. In his success though, he never forgot those less fortunate than himself. As we look up at the window when we leave the Minster, the story of the mustard maker is a good one upon which we can reflect.

The Bookseller's Tale

If you walk towards the main door of Croydon Minster and then turn right towards the gardens, you will soon see other parts of the church's history. You should be able to find the old war memorial. At the end of the First World War, this had been erected in front of the church where the car park is now, but was subsequently moved to its new place when various traffic schemes were introduced. A sign at the entrance to the gardens also tells you that this was the area which was, for hundreds of years, the churchyard.

After being formally closed for any further internments, the old tombstones were removed and many were used to create paths around the gardens and the church. As you walk around, you can pick out some information on those stones where the lettering has not eroded away. You can find names, ages and dates of death. All the stones were recorded and many have interesting stories to tell. Unfortunately, where the stones and tablets have been worn smooth, their commemorated names are lost to modern-day visitors.

One such stone commemorated the man who claimed to be the earliest printer in Croydon, a chap by the name of Timothy Harding. He died on 13th January 1825, aged 76. He had a tombstone on which his wife, Anne, was also recorded. She died on 3rd January 1840. By a coincidence, she was also 76 when she died.

Timothy Harding ran his business from a small office on the High Street. As well as a printer, he was a bookseller and stationer. He kept a circulating library containing many books, but often the trashiest romantic novels of the day! One source writes that his office was very small, his types the most old-fashioned, and his little printing press the most primitive. You might imagine what that little office might be like! Timothy was successful enough in business though to hire a helping hand. This person was described as a journeyman who, when there wasn't very much to do in the office, tended to the Hardings' garden. Back at the end of the eighteenth century and the beginning of the nineteenth when Timothy would have been working, there wouldn't have been a huge number of printing jobs. He was kept busy mostly though by printing the playbills for old Beverley, manager of the theatre, the summonses and other forms for the Court of Requests, and the bills and catalogues for an auctioneer.

Timothy did his best to generate further local interest in the print world by writing and publishing his own book. It was entitled *The Rural Beauties of Sanderstead.* To call it a book may misrepresent the work as one source called it a brochure. At any rate, it had a frontispiece, executed on wood, representing a lady in some distress, reclining by a weeping willow over a tomb in a churchyard. I wonder if he had in mind any of the tombs in the old churchyard when he created this illustration? It would have been just a short walk for him. The advertisement for the publication by Henry Sotheran in The Strand, London gives the work a price of 3 shillings and 6 pence. It also tells us that the book was sewn and was 8cto in size.

The alternate title of *Twelve Hours Perambulation* provides the curious reader with the exact nature of the "Beauties", namely the glorious countryside to be found around the village of Sanderstead as it was in those days. We are also told that this was one of the few book printed in Croydon at the time. Wouldn't it be fantastic if a long-lost copy was discovered in a trunk or in an attic somewhere?

By all accounts, Timothy was an eccentric gentleman. Often to be seen standing on the upper step in the doorway of his premises, he used his glasses as a means of non-verbal communication, staring over or through them as he saw fit. He was described a rather taciturn figure who was Pickwickian in appearance. Apparently he always wore nankeen breeches and white stockings, low shoes, light vest and a dark coat.

In an obituary written for *The Gentleman's magazine*, Harding was said to have died after a long and lingering illness which he bore patience. He was never known to complain. The writer adds that although Timothy was an eccentric person, he was not a bad man. The obituary was concluded with a statement that Harding was the oldest shopkeeper in Croydon.

It is such a shame that his memorial stone cannot be located in the gardens or around the side of the church building. Our Mr Harding seems quite a character. If you live or know people in Sanderstead, do keep searching for his book. That would really bring his tale to life.

Sunday Services

8.00am Eucharist
10.00am Sung Eucharist with Sunday Schools
6.30pm Choral Evensong

Weekday Services

Monday to Friday - 9.00am Morning Prayer
Monday - 12.00 noon Eucharist (except Bank Holidays)
Tuesday - 1.10pm Eucharist
5.30pm Choral Evensong (Term-time only)
Wednesday - 11.00am Eucharist (BCP)
5.30pm Choral Evensong (Term-time only)
Friday - 10.00am Eucharist
Saturday - 10.00am Eucharist

The Reverend Canon Colin J Luke Boswell
020 8688 8104
www.croydonminster.org
enquiries@croydonminster.org

Lightning Source UK Ltd.
Milton Keynes UK
UKOW06f0210100916

282613UK00002B/163/P